THEN & NOW

ESSEX AND MIDDLE RIVER

THEN & NOW

ESSEX AND MIDDLE RIVER

M. Linda Martinak and
Angela Martinak Sutherland

For our parents, George and Rita Martinak, who inspired us to be who we are today.

—LM and AS

ISBN 978-0-7385-5304-7

Library of Congress control number: 2007930068

Published by Arcadia Publishing
Charleston, South Carolina

Printed in the United States of America

Then and Now is a registered trademark and is used under license from Salamander Books Limited

For all general information contact Arcadia Publishing at:
Telephone 843-853-2070
Fax 843-853-0044
E-mail sales@arcadiapublishing.com

Visit us on the Internet at www.arcadiapublishing.com

On the Front Cover: Anyone visiting Essex and Middle River will inevitably ride along Eastern Avenue, the main road through the communities. The front cover shows the intersection of Eastern and Woodward Drive. Obvious major changes have occurred along Eastern, and this area is typical of those developments. The house in the foreground of the vintage photograph was owned by John B. Haut, one of the commissioners representing the area. Not far from his home was one of the first movie theaters in Essex, the Elektra. (Personal collection of the authors.)

On the Back Cover: Eastern Avenue has long been home to parades. This one shows two of the historic buildings in Essex. The left brick building is the current home of the Heritage Society of Essex and Middle River and was formerly the Essex Fire and Police Department. The building next to it was the first home to the Vigilant Volunteer Fire Department and later to the Vigilant Building Association. (Personal collection of the authors.)

Contents

Acknowledgments

The authors are indebted to a number of individuals who shared their firsthand information about the Essex–Middle River area, as well as their precious photographs from family collections. First and foremost, we are both very proud to be able to use the hard work of our father, George J. Martinak, who wrote the first book about the history of Essex in 1963 as one of his college papers at Essex Community College. While the book had a limited publication, there is a wealth of information in the small, collectible manuscript. We are very happy that we can share his writing with a larger audience through this work.

We thank Stan Piet from the Glenn L. Martin Aviation Museum for his patience in going through the archives for just the right photographs for this work and giving us permission to include those photographs. Piet was an invaluable source for us.

We also thank the Connelly family (Connelly Funeral Home), who not only shared their photographs with us but also became a drop-off point for us to pick up other pictures from longtime residents of Essex.

Thanks to Wayne Miskiewicz, classmate and friend, for his help with photographs from Maryland Marina and for his prompt response to our request. Additional thanks to the Zion Evangelical Lutheran Church and Aero Motors for their assistance.

Thanks, too, to Dave McCubbin for talking with us and for sharing our work with others so that we could gather more original source photographs for this project. Additional thanks go to the Heritage Society of Essex and Middle River. Thanks as well to Richard Parsons for his assistance in our preparations and also to Lightner Photography, Inc.

Lastly, we thank our families for their support while we put this work together and our publisher, Lauren Bobier, for keeping us on track when many things got in our way while trying to meet our deadline.

Unless otherwise noted, all modern images were taken by the authors.

References

Brooks, Neal and Richard Parsons. *Baltimore County Panorama*. Towson, MD: Baltimore County Library, 1988.

Freeman, Paul. *Abandoned and Little-Known Airfields: Maryland, Southeastern Baltimore County*. www.airfields-freeman.com/MD/Airfields_MD_Balt_SE.htm

Glenn L. Martin Maryland Aviation Museum.

Martinak, George J. *A Short History of Essex and Middle River*. Baltimore: self-published, 1963.

National Fire Sprinkler Association

Introduction

The beginnings of Essex and Middle River, part of eastern Baltimore County, can be traced back to the late 1700s and early 1800s and are largely because of the waterways that almost surround the region. Indeed, today much of the area is home to numerous marinas and water-related recreation activities.

The antecedents to what we now know as Essex and Middle River were tracts known as Hazard (1708), Outlet to Bushey Neck (1744), Littleworth (1753), Long's Addition (1746), Cox's Privilege (1776), and Cox's Marsh (1784). Paradise Farm, like some of the other tracts, was located near the area now known as Cox's Point. Eventually the Taylor family owned a significant acreage near Duck Creek, having purchased Hazard, Paradise, Littleworth, Cox's Privilege, and others. A patent was issued in 1860 as Paradise Resurveyed, which contained 1,218 acres. A stone marker stood at Mace Avenue near Franklin Avenue and showed the letters I. H. P., which was believed to mark the place where Hazard met Paradise. It may date to the year 1860. The marker remains there, although a similar one is now at the Heritage Society of Essex and Middle River.

While the boundaries of Essex and Middle River have always been somewhat elastic, with some counting them as one, others as separate, the original acreage was bounded by the Back River, Mace Avenue, Back River Neck Road, and Duck Creek. Today some will say that Essex includes areas to the west of Back River, including an area that came into existence primarily because of the establishment of the Eastpoint Shopping Center and the Eastern Rolling Mill. Middle River was often thought of as beginning at Stemmers Run Road and ending on the other side of the river at either Bowleys Quarters Road or the community of Chase. The discussion continues on the exact boundaries of Essex and Middle River.

At any rate, the region became home to some well-known industries and to some interesting visitors. Probably the best-known industry in the area was the Glenn L. Martin Company. Most longtime residents of Essex and Middle River will probably have had at least one member of their family work at the Martin plant, which was a major builder in the aviation industry.

The 1,260 acres for the aircraft plant was purchased in 1929 for Glenn L. Martin by an agent, W. A. Crenning. Although starting operations at the height of the Depression, the Martin plant prospered and began to hire those who were looking so desperately for work. For Martin, the plant was a turning point in his career. A sign at the end of the Middle River Bridge proclaimed the area as the "Aircraft Center of the East." Thanks mostly to the notoriety of the Glenn L. Martin company, the Middle River plant hosted such guests as Franklin D. Roosevelt, Charles A. Lindbergh, Orville Wright, Amelia Earhart, Harry S Truman, and Douglas "Wrongway" Corrigan.

With the growth of the Glenn L. Martin Company, there was likewise a growth in population and housing for the many workers who came to build planes for the war and after. Small communities in Middle River grew up with names like Aero Acres, Mars Estates, and Victory Villa. At the height of operations, the Martin Company employed 54,000 workers.

One can safely say that Martin was the real impetus for the continued growth of the region throughout World War II and the Korean War. Indeed, even after the wars ended, Martin had a huge impact on the aviation and space industry. It might be called the single most important element in community development in Essex and Middle River. We might only imagine how the area would have developed without the Glenn L. Martin Company. But as a large business goes, so goes the neighborhood. In the late 1960s, the company began huge layoffs and moving employees to their plants in other states. The community began a decline, which was also fueled by the 1957 fire in Essex, when the entire block of the major stores burned to the ground.

The block never really returned to its best days, and residents took their business to larger, enclosed malls while the block remained vacant. In more recent years, however, there have been efforts to revitalize Essex, and some of that has been successful. In Middle River, there is a move to encourage development. Old apartment buildings that had encouraged crime and drugs have been demolished. Parks and single-family homes have replaced those sites, and the area is beginning to have a more clean and polished look. New business is using some of the Glenn L. Martin property, a light rail station has been installed nearby along Eastern Avenue, and the new extension to Route 43 has been opened. That route is now being developed with industrial and manufacturing businesses, and the waterfront is now more available for visitors to enjoy.

Several things became apparent in preparing this manuscript. For one thing, Essex lost many of its businesses to fire and those businesses never recovered. Another notable fact was that it now appears that the county is making a serious effort to help the area reach its full potential. Lastly, the book has made the authors aware of how fragile an area can become when the citizens and the government do not nurture it. Essex and Middle River is being nurtured from the county. Now it is up to the citizens to be good stewards of their communities.

CHAPTER 1

Religion in Essex and Middle River

Zion Evangelical Lutheran Church, shown here in an 1866 photograph, can trace its origins back to pre–Civil War days. The congregation was made up primarily of German immigrants who were employed at the local iron works. Initially they gathered in the Howard Church on adjacent land. The second church was built in 1896 as Evangelical Zions Church. (Courtesy of Zion Evangelical Lutheran Church.)

Zion Evangelical Lutheran Parsonage was built by at least 1922 and was part of an ongoing growth in the parish. The building was a clapboard structure and was constructed next to the church cemetery, about 75 yards from the church. During that period of growth, the pastor was Henry Ellenberger, who served the congregation vigorously for 21 years. The building still stands today and houses the church office. (Courtesy of Zion Evangelical Lutheran Church.)

Zion Evangelical Lutheran Church, opened in 1867, was home for worshippers living near the Locust Grove Iron Furnace. A newer church was built on adjacent land in 1896 and is the still the location of the current church. Further renovations to the structure were made in the 1960s and later. The church continues to thrive today at the same location. During its early history, the church underwent several name changes, starting with the Free and Independent Evangelical Howard Congregation in 1865. (Courtesy of Zion Evangelical Lutheran Church.)

The first Catholic church in Middle River was Our Lady of Mount Carmel, where the first baptism was dated 1893. Early ministry of the church was carried out by the Redemptorist Fathers with help from St. Joseph's parish in Fullerton. Cardinal James Gibbons of Baltimore appointed Rev. Francis Flanagan pastor of the church in 1905. An elementary school staffed by the Sisters of St. Francis in opened in 1927, and a high school opened its doors in 1959. Both schools remain in operation today. (Courtesy of *A Short History of Essex and Middle River*.)

As the population of Essex and Middle River continued to grow, Our Lady of Mount Carmel soon became overcrowded, and the parish was divided into two additional Catholic parishes—Our Lady Queen of Peace in 1953, which began ministry to those living to the northeast near the White Marsh area, and St. Clare's in 1956, where the school was staffed as a mission of the Mercy Sisters of Kells, Ireland, no other order of nuns being available. (Courtesy of St. Clare's Church; photographer, Charles J. Cignatta.)

St. Clare's Parish Rectory was originally housed in an old home that was on the property of the parish grounds. When the church opened in 1956, Rev. Albert T. Stallings was appointed pastor. He was later joined by several assistants, who all made the house their home. Renovations were made to the building, and it served its purpose until 1970, when the priests moved to their new brick residence behind the existing structure. (Courtesy of St. Clare's Church.)

St. Stephen's African Methodist Episcopal Church, at the corner of Back River Neck Road and Stemmers Run Road, was established around the 1870s. The church, originally a log structure with siding, was rebuilt several times since those early days, including in 1907 and 1972. It still stands at the same location, known as by locals as Josenhans Corner, where one of the first two general stores in town was located. Led today by Rev. William A. Gray III, it is the oldest African American church in Essex. (Courtesy of Paul Blitz from the Essex and Middle River Heritage Society.)

St. John's Evangelical Lutheran Church laid its cornerstone in September 1913. The church, at the corner of George Avenue and Franklin Avenue, was ministered to by the Reverend C. E. W. Hartlage, pastor until 1929, first paid at a salary of $5 per month. The older photograph shows the St. John's steeple in the background around 1927. Today the church has expended considerably. Since 1998, Pastor Lans Alexis has led St. John's at its larger facility at 522 and 524 Franklin Avenue. (Personal collection of the authors.)

The Essex Methodist Church was built in 1913 at the southwest corner of Eastern Avenue and Taylor Avenue. In 1915, the church rented its basement for classrooms for the Essex Elementary School. The church was later demolished and relocated to make way for stores. The original site is now used as a county government multipurpose services building. The current location of the Essex Methodist Church is at the corner of Woodward Drive and Maryland Avenue. (Courtesy of *A Short History of Essex and Middle River*.)

Our Lady of Mount Carmel Church Rectory was built in the same mission style as the church. An anomaly design for the area, all of the Mount Carmel buildings were finished on the outside in stucco and painted pink. The buildings remained that color until sometime in the 1990s. The rectory at one point in time housed as many as five priests—a period when several priests served each parish in the archdiocese. This is certainly not the case today. (Personal collection of authors.)

One of the first churches established in the region was Orems Methodist Church in 1773. Christopher Duke, one of those deeding the church property, refused to subscribe to the Revolutionary Oath and was fined for his independent views. While confiscation of property was common in these cases, no such action was taken, though preaching was restricted and fines were levied. (Personal collection of the authors.)

The First Baptist Church of Essex has its origins as a mission of the Tabernacle Baptist Church on Bennett Road. Tabernacle Church began meeting in 1947 under the name of Tabernacle Baptist Chapel at the old Hiway Movie Theatre near Middle River Bridge. After a new Tabernacle Church was built on Bennett, two more congregations sprang from it, one being First Baptist on Mace Avenue. Prior to the present building, First Baptist met in a small building in the 1950s behind the Connelly Funeral Home. (Courtesy of Tablernacle Baptist Church.)

CHAPTER 2

EDUCATION AND COMMERCE

As the region grew, so did the need for community services. Harry Guttenberger opened his general store at the intersection of Eastern and Mace Avenues in 1910. His only competition at that time was a store owned by Frederick Josenhans several miles east and built in 1907. Guttenberger served as a purveyor of groceries, a center for trial magistrate (equivalent to a courtroom where a judge makes decision), coroner, and one-man police force. Guttenberger was the proverbial jack-of-all-trades. (Courtesy of *A Short History of Essex and Middle River*.)

Considered to be the first residence built in Essex, the old Schuster house is located at the corner of Dorsey and Taylor Avenues. Since that time, it has served as a private residence. The home was enlarged to the rear some years ago. In addition to the Schusters, the home became a residence for one of the Essex dentists, Dr. Charles McGarry. It is also the location where the design for the first St. John's Evangelical Lutheran Church on Franklin Avenue was developed. (Courtesy of *A Short History of Essex and Middle River*.)

In 1915, Essex residents relied on the services of the Vigilant Volunteer Fire Department. Original equipment was horse drawn. The first mechanized equipment was added in 1914. Housed at 518 Eastern Avenue, the company moved next door in 1921 and became a paid fire service for the Essex community. The original building, still standing today, had also been home to the Vigilant Building Association for many years before it was used by a private business. (Courtesy of *A Short History of Essex and Middle River*.)

Over the years, the fire department remained on Eastern Avenue but underwent expansion to include more space for equipment and added room for the police department and the local jail. In 1970, the fire department relocated to Myrth Avenue, where it was enlarged and from which easier access to the community was available. Their previous home on Eastern Avenue became the museum site for the Heritage Society of Essex and Middle River. (Courtesy of the Baltimore County Library.)

The Connelly Funeral Home, founded by John Gordon Connelly Sr., opened for business on Eastern Avenue in 1924. Sons John Gordon Jr. and Charles O. Connelly Sr. moved the business to its current location on Mace Avenue in 1961. The business is still owned and operated by John Sr.'s grandsons Terry Sr. and Greg and great-grandson Terry Jr. The original location of the establishment is now a real estate business and was formerly legislative offices. (Courtesy of Greg Connelly, Connelly Funeral Home.)

The first building to serve as a school in Essex (starting in 1913) was "a bungalow on the southeast corner of Taylor Avenue and Eastern Avenue." Two more classrooms were used in 1915 in the basement of the Essex Methodist Church. In 1916, a four-room school was erected at Dorsey Avenue and Woodward Drive, shown in the photograph. A graduating exercise was held in 1917 and included two girls. In 1920, a second four-room building was added to the site, plus some portable classrooms. (Courtesy of *A Short History of Essex and Middle River*.)

Following the use of portable buildings and the construction of another four-room schoolhouse, Essex was still in need of more space. Thus in 1925, a larger school was constructed at Mace and Franklin Avenues. Further expansion and renovation was necessary in recent years when the original Mace Avenue building was razed to make room for the current building, leaving the main entrance intact as a historical record of its previous existence. (Courtesy of *A Short History of Essex and Middle River*.)

As the school population increased, St. Clare's opened its doors in 1956. The first building housed eight classrooms and the basement church. The school opened with grades one through three and continued to add a new grade each year until all eight grades were incorporated. Though children were initially taught by temporary faculty, the Mercy Sisters from Ireland arrived to staff the school as a mission. Pastor Albert T. Stallings had approached some 58 American orders of nuns before finally finding the nuns from Kells. (Courtesy of St. Clare's Church.)

Our Lady of Mount Carmel Church built its elementary school in 1925. The first class of students included six boys and five girls. Pictured here are the graduating students in the class of 1930. Shown with the students are Msgr. Nicholas Jaselli, pastor of the parish, and Sr. Mary Philomena of the Order of St. Francis, the first principal of the school. At that time, the school contained four classrooms and an auditorium. (Personal collection of the authors.)

In 1940, the first Essex School building (the Taylor Land Company bungalow) was torn down to make room for a shopping center. The group of stores in the strip mall that was built remained in existence until a fire destroyed them in August 1957. The 10-alarm blaze resulted in almost $1 million in damages. Considered the worst fire in Baltimore County history, it dealt a blow to the Essex business community from which it has never truly recovered. (Courtesy of the National Fire Sprinkler Association.)

One of the early restaurants in Essex, Kalb's at 424 Eastern Avenue rated themselves on a postcard as having "a reputation for the finest foods, appetizingly prepared and served in a setting of air-conditioned comfort and pleasure." At that time, a lunch could be had for a mere 50¢ and dinner for 75¢. Today the restaurant is still in operation, although it has changed its ownership and its name, now trading as Uncle Eddies. (Personal collection of the authors.)

One of the businesses springing up in Essex was the Essex Bakery. Owned and operated by the Paul Matthai family, the bakery was one of the few businesses not to develop on the main thoroughfare, Eastern Avenue. The bakery opened in 1921 on Franklin Avenue, later moving to Eastern near Woodward Drive. Bakery goods were originally delivered by horse and wagon. The original house remained in the Matthai family into the late 20th century and is now a private residence. (Courtesy of *A Short History of Essex and Middle River*.)

Foulke's Garage and car dealership was originally located in the 600 block of Eastern Avenue near the former Sunny Surplus store and the Domino Pizza store. It later moved eastward to a larger, more comfortable location. The photograph shows the location on Eastern across from what had been an early amusement park. Aero Motors, which had been on Martin Boulevard in Middle River, acquired the dealership and moved its operations to the Foulke's building. (Courtesy of Joe Eikenberg Jr., Aero Motors.)

In 1944, public library service in Baltimore County began in Middle River in a small room in the Federal Housing Authority's recreation building at Martin Boulevard and Compass Road. Service predated the Baltimore County Library system by four years. The library was the first to offer a phonograph record collection thanks to the generosity of the Glenn L. Martin Company. In 1958, the library moved to a new building, and in 1968, it suffered from a fire, losing furniture and books to the tune of $25,000. (Courtesy of Baltimore County Library.)

The Essex Library has a long history of moves. The first lending library was opened in a classroom of Essex School in 1947 and moved later that year to an apartment at 42 Warren Road. Not part of the Baltimore County Library system at the time, the library was under the care of Frances Bourne. The next move was to South Taylor Avenue beneath Reads Drugs in 1950. Two more moves included Maryland Avenue (the shorter building shown in the photograph) and to the present location in Middlesex Shopping Center. (Personal collection of the authors.)

Overlea Bank opened in Essex in 1925. The bank sold stamps in small denominations to the children savers and supplied them with cards to which the stamps were affixed. When the cards filled, the youngsters would take them to the bank and have them deposited to their accounts. The bank was absorbed by Union Trust in 1927 and closed in 1933. It reopened in 1954 and eventually moved to Eastern Avenue and Stuart Street. It is now Wachovia Bank, at the same location. (Personal collection of the authors.)

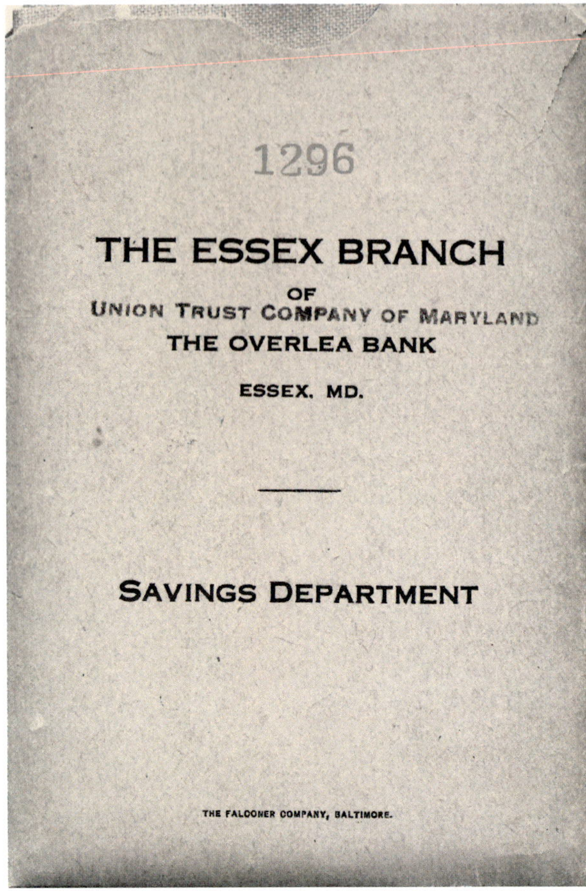

The only site in Essex and Middle River currently on the National Historic Trust list is Ballestone Mansion. The building, now owned by Baltimore County, is on the land adjacent to Rocky Point Golf Course on Back River Neck Road. Several alterations and additions were made to the *c.* 1800 house. Efforts have been made to completely renovate the site, and it now serves as a handsome example of a "large farmhouse of the 1870's and 1880's," according to the Web site of the Maryland Historical Trust. (Courtesy of the Baltimore County Library.)

One of the more elegant homes, Bauernschmidt Manor off Turkey Point Road was the summer residence of the owners of the Bauernschmidt Beer Company in Baltimore. The house is located on a peninsula between Hog Pen Creek and Middle River, obviously a place to catch the sea breezes during hot summers. Still located on the original property and having changed hands and had renovations, the manor is now serving as a bed-and-breakfast. (Courtesy of the Baltimore County Library.)

CHAPTER 3

INDUSTRY AND COMMUNITY GROWTH

Franklin D. Roosevelt visited the Glenn L. Martin Company in September 1940. He was greeted at the main gate by Glenn L. Martin himself (front passenger seat), and they drove through the plant while Martin pointed out the details of the navy P5M flying boat under construction in "B" building. Maryland governor Herbert R. O'Conor (next to Roosevelt in back seat) accompanied Martin and Roosevelt on the visit. (Courtesy of *A Short History of Essex and Middle River*.)

Largely responsible for the exponential growth in the Essex and Middle River area, the Glenn L. Martin Company opened its doors on 1,260 acres in 1929. During the early years of the company and over the period of World War II, the Martin Company built, according to the Glenn L. Martin Maryland Aviation Museum brochure, "over 80 different types of aircraft, totaling more than 11,000 planes." Some of the Martin seaplanes (which they called flying boats) could be launched from the Martin Lagoon behind the main plant. (Courtesy of the Glenn L. Martin Aviation Museum.)

In a large part because of the aviation industry at Glenn L. Martin, the area around the factory grew rapidly. Communities named for the aviation industry sprang up, including Aero Acres and Victory Villa. Street names included those of airplane parts, including Fuselage, Compass, and Altimeter. Many of the buildings, pre-fabs or small bungalows, remain today. Many have expanded to include a second floor or addition off the back of the house. (Courtesy of the Glenn L. Martin Aviation Museum.)

As Martin grew, so went the community of Aero Acres. In addition to shopping facilities and the USO building, a movie theater was also opened in 1942. The usherettes wore uniforms with an aviation theme. First-run movies were shown at the location with ample parking. Patrons could walk under sheltered sidewalks to stay out of inclement weather. With the advent of this theater, the *Martin Star* magazine claimed, "filmstars wired congratulations on the opening." The current site is now a supermarket. (Courtesy of the Glenn L. Martin Aviation Museum.)

In 1947, the cornerstone of the Essex War Memorial was laid. Official dedication came on May 2, 1948. The granite monument recognizes the 19 men from Essex who gave their lives for our country in the Second World War. Inside the cornerstone of the monument are the names of those men, a Bible, and other mementos. The dedication was marked by a grand parade and approximately 5,000 people attending. The speaker for the occasion was John N. Maguire. (Personal collection of the authors.)

The USO building in Aero Acres was dedicated in 1942. Celebrity attendees included Joe E. Brown, Maryland governor Herbert R. O'Conor, U.S. Speaker of the House Sam Rayburn, and Glenn L. Martin. Entertainment was provided by the Kenwood High School Glee Club. The building was located near the corner of Martin Boulevard and Compass Road. Today the site is a senior center. Originally the site included lounges and reading and music rooms. Parties, dances, and basketball games were held there. (Courtesy of the Glenn L. Martin Aviation Museum.)

The privately owned Martin airport was established in 1939. At the center of operations was the control tower, still in use today. In its early days, the tower controlled the operations of army and civilian test pilots taking off from the Middle River facility. During that time, there were also six hangars and the main administration building at the location. Today the tower is central to the Martin State Airport, which has now added corporate hangars near the original six. (Courtesy of the Glenn L. Martin Aviation Museum.)

As the working population at the Martin plant increased, it became necessary for more housing to be built for them. In addition to Aero Acres and Victory Villa, Stansbury Estates was built just south of the main plant on Wilson Point Road. The complex was considered to be "outstanding, low-cost housing." The *Martin Star* magazine announced the soon-to-be built 1,200 units in its April 1942 issue, citing that Middle River would soon become "the second largest city in Maryland." (Courtesy of the Glenn L. Martin Aviation Museum.)

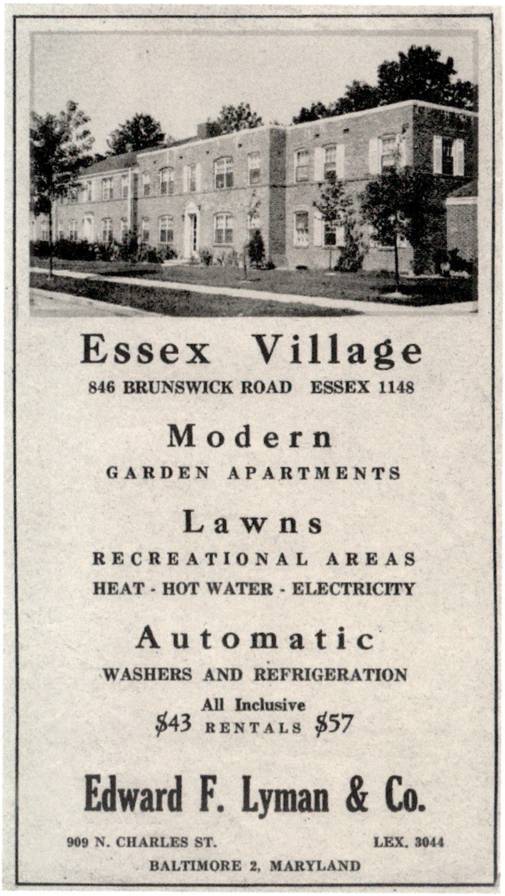

Essex Village was one of several apartment complexes built to house the increasing wartime population in the region. Located off South Marlyn Avenue and Brunswick Road, housing was available from $43 to $57 per month. The price included such amenities as heat, janitor service, hot and cold running water, electricity, and recreational areas. Garden apartments were also available for the residents. (Personal collection of the authors.)

The Glenn L. Martin Company has probably had the greatest impact on the growth as well as the decline in the region in population and business life. While at one time it had employed as many as 53,000 workers, numerous employees were transferred to plants in Orlando, Denver, and California. The plant changed its direction, becoming the Martin Marietta Company and, later, Lockheed Martin. Today's Middle River plant employs only a small percentage of the number who once worked there. (Then photograph, personal collection of the authors; now photograph, courtesy of the Glenn L. Martin Aviation Museum.)

During the war years, there was great concern over the security of the Glenn L. Martin Company and its operations. Frequent mention was made in the *Martin Star*, the plant newspaper, about the need for secrecy. One such note was "Shh! Telling a Friend May Mean Telling An Enemy." Pictured is a member of today's private security force. (Then photograph, courtesy of the Glenn L. Martin Aviation Museum; now photograph, courtesy of Karen McClellan.)

In the midst of development in Essex and Middle River, one frequently found unpaved roads, such as this one, Margaret Avenue. Some roads, such as Woodward Drive, were paved part of the way and then continued as a narrower, cinder-covered thoroughfare into the undeveloped woods. Looking north in this photograph, one can just see the Essex Fire Department on the main highway, Eastern Avenue. (Courtesy of Heritage Society of Essex and Middle River.)

In the late 1940s and early 1950s, Essex continued its development with the construction of small two- or three-bedroom homes. This location looking south on Taylor Avenue from Virginia Avenue is a prime example of how the center of Essex boomed. Notice that in the early photograph, one can just barely see Back River. No such sight is now available, as homes not only line Taylor Avenue but also the banks of the river. (Personal collection of the authors.)

As late as the early 1950s, a seaplane base was still operating on the shores of Back River. Seaplane rides were available for a fee. Owned and operated by Harry Carl, the base was also inhabited by a large Chesapeake Bay retriever who gently greeted those entering the area. Located on Riverside Drive at the end of Margaret Avenue, the site is today the home of Riverside Marina and Sales. (Personal collection of the authors.)

The Glenn L. Martin Company was not the only aviation business in Middle River. In 1947, Diffendahl Airport (later sold and renamed Eastern Airport and then Essex Skypark) opened not far from the Martin plant on Back River Neck Road. The airport had two grass runways, one northwest-southeast and the other northeast-southwest. Also provided at this location was a seaplane base south of Witch Coat Point. The airport has since been purchased by Baltimore County. (Courtesy of www.airfields-freeman.com.)

In the early 1940s, the Pennsylvania Railroad operated some train services to the Essex and Middle River region. A Pennsylvania Railroad station was in use located between Orems and Stemmers Run Roads. The Stemmers Run station building had been used by AMTRAK for maintenance purposes. It now appears to be abandoned. The site was a prime location for local residents when the train carrying the casket of Robert F. Kennedy passed by on the way to Washington, D.C. (Courtesy of the Baltimore County Library.)

The eastern area of Baltimore County continued to grow rapidly during the postwar years. Yearly there was an Independence Day Parade, usually along several blocks of the main street, Eastern Avenue. During the early 1950s, the parade often included military units from the army and navy, along with military bands and vehicles. Today this same corner at Stuart Street and Eastern is home to four businesses and parades that include few if any military units. (Personal collection of the authors.)

After the Essex fire in 1957, some businesses continued to operate in the middle of town. Unfortunately, fire took another toll in the early 1960s. The fire destroyed the Word of Faith Church, which had as its home the old Elektra Theatre. Also suffering was the Catherine's Florist business. Operating next to those locations was longtime business Milke's Hardware, with great old creaky wooden floors and bins for nails and other sundries. Today the site of Milke's is home to an insurance agency. (Personal collection of the authors.)

Vigilant Building Association began its banking business in the old Vigilant Volunteer Fire Department building in 1927, located next to the current Heritage Society of Essex and Middle River. The basic outline of the original building remains there. The bank has now moved to a much larger and imposing edifice at the corner of Eastern Avenue and Woodward Drive. Locally owned and operated since its inception, the bank encouraged residents to invest their savings in local mortgages. (Personal collection of the authors.)

Services and transportation were not the only requirements for a growing community. Recreational opportunities were also needed in the eastern end of the county. One such location for sun and fun was and is Rocky Point Park, located off Back River Neck Road. The park, now owned by Baltimore County, remains a place for swimming and includes a sailing center. The gate to the park still stands as sentry to the park entrance. (Courtesy of Paul Blitz from the Heritage Society of Essex and Middle River.)

For community members who wanted recreational sports on a year-round basis, Essex provided the Essex Bowling Centre, located next to the fire department across from the shopping center on Margaret Avenue. Early on, the duckpin bowling center used the services of pin-boys. Later automatic pin-setters were added. Bowling was available both on the main entry floor as well as downstairs. After the building was demolished, the B. Bugatch Furniture Store opened there. Today CVS occupies most of the block. (Personal collection of the authors.)

In the early 1960s, Essex suffered another fire and the end of another business. The Eastway Movie Theatre (formerly the New Essex) blaze occurred in the early hours of a January morning. It took three alarms and 10 county fire departments to extinguish the difficult fire while hampered by cold temperatures and heavy winds. The theater was a total loss and was never rebuilt. The site today houses a building used by the Teamsters as a union hall. (Personal collection of the authors.)

Entertainment for the area came in many forms. Little traffic during snowstorms allowed county police to close some roads in Essex so that the local youth could take advantage of a snow day. This scene on Myrth Avenue was one such location for the fun. On the road, drivers would find a sign blocking their progress. It was labeled "Road Closed—Children Coasting." This recreational situation is not likely to happen today on the widened and much busier Myrth Avenue. (Personal collection of the authors.)

Ed and Catherine Yake owned Catherine's Florist. Their store, barely seen here on the left behind the crowds watching the parade, was located on Eastern Avenue near the Vigilant Bank building, the first firehouse in Essex. The Yakes left Essex in 1962 amid a great gathering of Essex residents and business leaders. The florist was sold to another owner and eventually moved farther down Eastern Avenue and nearer to Mace Avenue. (Personal collection of the authors.)

The Back River Trolley was part of the Back and Middle River Line. The trolley was a nine-bench, open, single-track electric car used by the United Railways in Essex. The trolley ran only to Back River in 1895 but expanded its service to Middle River three years later. The trolley ride was described in *A Short History of Essex and Middle River* as "one of the most pleasant country rides to be found." Today the region is served by bus courtesy of the Baltimore Metropolitan Transit Administration. (Courtesy of the collection of George J. Martinak.)

Some businesses that started in Essex have not only remained there but have flourished today. Salvo Auto Parts is one of those that has continued to thrive over the years since it began business in 1935. Originally located at the well-known Josenhans Corner at Old Eastern Avenue and Stemmers Run Road, the business remains at that location. Salvo now has eight other stores located throughout the north and east side of Baltimore County. (Courtesy of a 1930s area map, publisher unknown.)

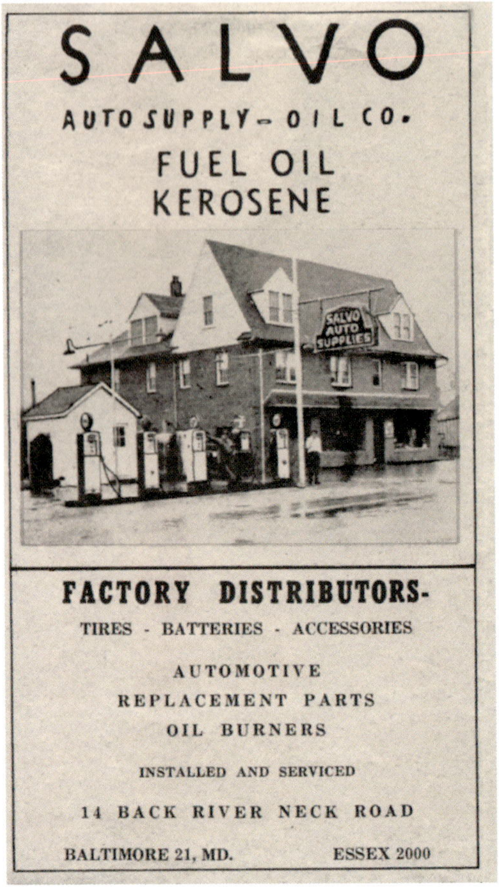

CHAPTER 4

Growth, Decline, and Revitalization

Some Things Change

Standing on a makeshift platform behind the "A" building at the Glenn L. Martin Company, Douglas "Wrongway" Corrigan (right) spoke to workers in 1938. Corrigan told workers about how it felt to fly 3,150 miles nonstop east while he thought he was heading west by following the wrong end of the compass needle. His original destination was California. He landed in Ireland. Glenn L. Martin stands on the left. (Personal collection of the authors.)

Eastern Avenue, now Route 150, runs right through the heart of the Essex and Middle River business district. Starting in downtown Baltimore, it ends on the east end in the community of Chase. The corner of Woodward Drive and Eastern Avenue would have been considered the east end of the Essex business area at the time of the photograph. The road now is significantly wider than in those early days and carries traffic that none could have imagined when it was first established. (Personal collection of the authors.)

With the rapid growth of the Glenn L. Martin Company, numerous housing units were constructed to house the workers. Communities and community services were part of the company's plans for its employees. Housing was built near the large airplane plant, and often shuttle service to work was supplied. These houses, once near Martin Boulevard, were recently razed for a newer and larger community. (Courtesy of the Glenn L. Martin Aviation Museum.)

For many years, the Riverdale Apartments were located at the west side of Middle River Bridge. Advertised as renting for only $50 per month, the housing was also built during the early years of work at the Martin Company. The buildings remained low-cost housing until the late 1990s. They have since been removed for single-family dwellings, as part of the area's revitalization efforts. (Personal collection of the authors.)

Building airplanes during wartime required lots of security, as evidenced by the photograph on page 51. This private guard had his duty at the Middle River bridge. Today he would have a much larger span to watch over. The bridge has been expanded to six lanes and has been modernized for both practical and aesthetic reasons. The area is now focusing on its location near the Chesapeake Bay, a playground for visitors and a place for water recreation. (Courtesy of Paul Blitz from the Heritage Society of Essex and Middle River.)

According to www.marylandmarina.net, Maryland Marina started its business as "a small boat manufacturing plant" in 1946. Located on Frog Mortar Creek, off Middle River and close to the Chesapeake Bay, the business has remained in the family since it opened. Today the business focuses its work on marina operations, having ended its boatbuilding in 1967. The marina has been in the able hands of the Miskiewicz family for four generations. It provides a protected harbor for as many as 360 boats. (Courtesy of Wayne Miskiewicz.)

The southeast corner of Eastern Avenue and Taylor Avenue was the location of Taylor Land Company, which had built a sample home to use as its office. The building was later used as the first Essex School, which also rented basement space at the Essex Methodist Church. In 1940, the building was demolished to build a shopping center. At that time, the corner became home to Reads Drug Store. Reads was one of the stores lost in the 1957 fire. (Courtesy of *A Short History of Essex and Middle River*.)

Across the street from Reads Drug Store was Juliano's corner. In early Essex business life, Thomas Juliano ran a local bar. A barbershop shared the block with a dry goods store (the Globe). The Globe eventually became a flooring store. All of these businesses are now gone for progress and revitalization. A large CVS store and parking lot now are at the corner. (Personal collection of the authors.)

Visitors have been welcomed with signs since the community began. One, of course, advertised the opportunity to buy a lot in an up-and-coming neighborhood. Later visitors and residents were greeted by a sign at the Back River Bridge welcoming them to Essex and Middle River and sponsored not only by the Chamber of Commerce, but also the Rotary, the Kiwanis, the Lions, and the Optimists. Today, with emphasis on new growth and development, the welcome includes "Gateway to the Chesapeake." (Courtesy of *A Short History of Essex and Middle River*.)

By 1975, some of the fire-damaged 500 block of Eastern Avenue had begun to come back to life. In the background of this vintage photograph, one can see some of the businesses that had made their home in Essex. In the current photograph, it is apparent that the businesses in the earlier photograph are now gone. The block then included Maryland National Bank, Pappy's Beef and Beer, Charles Bootery (a shoe store), and a supermarket that was primarily entered from the lower, back level of the building. The modern photograph shows a very different scene. (Personal collection of the authors.)

Efforts to return the Back River shoreline to conditions similar to those that met visitors in the late 1800s began with the establishment of Cox's Point Park, at the end of Riverside Drive on the west end of Essex. The park is located between Back River and Duck Creek. Today it provides an area for locals to picnic, fish, and launch their boats. The point bears the last surviving name of a land grant for Essex. (Personal collection of the authors.)

The land just adjacent to the shore of Back River was once home to places like Hollywood Park and a number of local watering holes that satisfied folks from the city, where there was a Sunday "closing law." Hollywood Park burned down in 1921. Later the Eastern Amusement Park opened nearby on a site that has continued to be used for recreation. The site became a roller rink and is now home to a bingo hall. While buildings changed, the purpose has remained the same. (Courtesy of Paul Blitz from the Heritage Society of Essex and Middle River.)

With baby boomers in plentiful supply, Essex and Middle River began to require more schools. Eastern Technical High School was founded in the 1970s; the school is located on Mace Avenue, not far from Kenwood High. Its early name was Eastern Vocational and Technical High School. The school has long been known for its rigorous admission process and was recently recognized as a Blue Ribbon School. (Courtesy of *Essex Times*.)

Those who have lived in the Essex and Middle River area for any length of time can tell you exactly where Josenhans Corner is. The answer is at the corner of Old Eastern Avenue and Back River Neck Road. The building owned by Frederick Josenhans was actually the first general store in the area, predating Guttenberger's by several years. Since those early years, it has housed numerous businesses, including a laundromat. (Courtesy of *Baltimore County Panorama*.)

In 1963, the Essex Improvement Association built and donated a community garden to the Essex Community College (ECC), then housed at the corner of Dorsey Avenue and Woodward Drive. Plants and materials for the garden were given by Essex residents, businesses, organizations, and the Baltimore County Department of Recreation and Parks. A formal dedication of the garden was held in May and attended by then ECC president Moses Koch and community members. The garden has been replaced by a sign for the senior center, the building's current occupants. (Personal collection of the authors.)

The Essex Police Department was originally housed in the same building in which the fire department resided on Eastern Avenue. The station not only had cells for prisoners, but it also was the location for the district court. When the fire department relocated to their current location on Myrth Avenue, the police moved in 1973 to their present home on North Marlyn Avenue. The number of police employees in the district has more than doubled since the time the department moved. (Courtesy of the Baltimore County Library.)

Identified by the county surveyors as the first boundary marker of a tract known as Hines' Purchase, the granite stone marked about 261 acres extending to Back River and Northeast Creek. The land was part of a parcel know as Come By Chance, surveyed in 1694, and was an early parcel of Essex itself. Today the stone marks just the beginning of a long Essex journey. (Courtesy of *A Short History of Essex and Middle River*.)

Established in the 1920s, a clothing factory, always known as the "sewing factory," was established at Franklin Avenue and Stuart Street. Seamstresses worked there well into the nights. Local information was that shirts were being manufactured there. Later the building became the Toby Manufacturing Company. Today no name sign remains, but there is still a sign stating "seamstresses needed." Operations appear to continue there. (Personal collection of the authors.)

Walter Ward ran his barbershop at the corner of an alley behind the 400 block of Eastern and Taylor Avenues. Though he started his business at another location in Essex, the building in the picture served him well from 1958 until he stopped barbering. Ward came to Essex from Salem, West Virginia. Local residents and businesses near the alley came to blows with the Essex revitalization committee in 1979, when there were plans to widen the alley. (Courtesy of the *Avenue* newspaper.)

Bengie's Drive-In movie theater opened its outdoor doors in the Bowleys Quarters neighborhood of Middle River on June 6, 1966. Featuring the largest movie screen in the United States at 52 feet by 120 feet, it has long featured first-run films and advertises triple features on weekends. The location has been a draw to the region ever since its opening and is a favorite with the locals. (Courtesy of Bengies Drive-In Web site, www.bengies.com.)

As the county grew, there was a serious need for higher education opportunities for the residents of the eastern region. In 1957, the Baltimore County Board of Education founded Essex Community College. First classes were held at Kenwood High School in the evenings, but rapid enrollment resulted in the college using the old grammar school on Dorsey Avenue and Woodford Drive in 1961. The college moved to Rossville in 1968. Today Essex Community College is part of the Community College of Baltimore County. (Personal collection of the authors.)

The Essex Post Office has moved twice since the 1950s. Originally located in the 500 block of Eastern Avenue, it moved to the corner of Maryland and South Taylor Avenues. The office at Maryland Avenue had an L-shaped counter with about five or six windows for service. The inner workings of the office were in plain sight of the customers, and usually all of the windows were available for service. Because of the need for more space, the post office moved again to its current space behind the 400 block of Eastern Avenue, still on Taylor. (Personal collection of authors.)

In the early days of Essex, many roads were unpaved or unfinished. Some would start, peter out, and start again a block or two from the other part of the road. George Avenue is a prime example of this pattern. The road was discontinuous in three different locations. In 1959, part of the problem was addressed with the addition of a new part of the road and new residences north of Gerries Avenue. This vintage photograph shows the work as it began. (Personal collection of the authors.)

The United Railway and Electric Company Streetcar Barn was located near the west side of Back River bridge, along Eastern Avenue near Moffitt Avenue. Streetcars were later replaced for public transportation by buses from the Baltimore Transit Company, which ran farther to the east down to the Bengie's area of the county. The site on which the barn was located is now home to the Back River Wastewater Treatment Plant, built in 1912. (Personal collection of the authors.)

The Essex Library, although not a bookmobile, has certainly been a mobile entity. One of its moves was to a location on South Taylor, where the Chesapeake and Potomac Telephone Company had been. Later it moved to a newer and larger space on Maryland Avenue, next to the post office. At that time, it did indeed run a bookmobile as well. As its collection grew larger, the library moved to its current home in the Middlesex Shopping Center farther east. (Personal collection of the authors.)

The only high school close enough to serve the Essex and Middle River region was Kenwood High School. Originally in 1932, it stood outside the Essex and Middle River boundaries on Old Philadelphia Road. That building now houses Golden Ring Middle School. Kenwood moved inside the Essex boundaries to its present location on Stemmers Run Road in 1955. Further expansion of Kenwood High is currently in progress. (Courtesy of the Baltimore County Library.)

Like some of the other historical locations in Essex, the Elektra Theatre, then used as a church revival center, suffered its demise by fire. In 1963, the building, some apartments, and Catherine's Florist were totally lost. Six firefighters were injured. The cause of the fire was determined to be children playing with matches. The children were only 9 and 10 years old. Catherine's Florist, then owned by Cora Menefee, relocated to its current location on Eastern Avenue. (Courtesy of an unknown local newspaper.)

Middlesex Shopping Center began operations in 1955. Although the series of stores in the mall have changed and changed again, the mall continues to be well received by the residents of Essex and Middle River. Along with a complete remake of the facade and new stores, the mall is also home to a large grocery store, which once started out as Food Fair. (Personal collection of the authors.)

When you say Miami Beach, you generally think of Florida. Of course, if you live in Bowleys Quarters, you think "just down the road." Once privately owned, the beach is run by the Baltimore County Recreation and Parks Department. It consists of 59 acres of land that fronts the Chesapeake Bay across from Hart and Millers Islands. In addition to a small beach, the park also has a pavilion and playground. Trails are also available for those who come to Miami (Middle River, that is). (Courtesy of Baltimore County Library.)